In this book, we look to the stars and explore the planets, asteroids, moons and comets that fill our solar system.

LADYBIRD BOOKS

UK | USA | Canada | Ireland | Australia
India | New Zealand | South Africa

Ladybird Books is part of the Penguin Random House group of companies
whose addresses can be found at global.penguinrandomhouse.com.

www.penguin.co.uk   www.puffin.co.uk   www.ladybird.co.uk

Penguin
Random House
UK

First published 2021
001
Copyright © Ladybird Books Ltd, 2021
Printed in China
The authorized representative in the EEA is Penguin Random House Ireland,
Morrison Chambers, 32 Nassau Street, Dublin D02 YH68
A CIP catalogue record for this book is available from the British Library
ISBN: 978–0–241–41713–3
All correspondence to:
Ladybird Books
Penguin Random House Children's
One Embassy Gardens, 8 Viaduct Gardens
London SW11 7BW

The Solar System

A Ladybird Book

Written by Stuart Atkinson
with space consultant, Dr Suzanne Imber

Illustrated by Brave the Woods

Looking up on a clear night

There are many fascinating and beautiful things in the night sky. In towns and cities, the lights of buildings, cars and street lights limit what people can see, as only the brightest objects in the sky will show up. It is amazing how much more there is to see at night under a darker sky.

A dark sky is illuminated by thousands of twinkling stars. The brightness of a star depends on its power and its distance from Earth. If a star is a particular temperature or age, it may appear to be in colour – red, blue or white. If you see a very bright star that isn't twinkling, it is almost certainly a planet – either Venus, Mars or Jupiter.

A shooting star might also skip across the sky and, despite its name, it is not really a star at all. It is a streak of light caused by space dust or small rocks, called "meteoroids", flying through the atmosphere and then burning up.

The night sky is also home to the Moon. The Moon appears to change shape from night to night in a process called "the lunar cycle" – it can be a bright, white ball, a smiling crescent or completely invisible!

The night sky does not look the same every night. As the Earth spins, the stars, the Moon and planets appear to move, rising and setting in an ever-changing pattern.

Stars

A long time ago, people thought that stars were holes in the sky, or glittering crystals hanging above the Earth. Today, we know that stars are actually huge balls of burning hot gas that exist in space.

The closest star to Earth is the Sun. The Earth's Sun, which shines during the day, is a lot like the stars we see at night, but it is much closer to Earth. This is why its warmth can be felt whenever it appears in the sky. All of the stars in the night sky are like distant suns, and they burn just as bright!

Scientists don't use miles or kilometres to measure the distance between Earth and other stars in the galaxy, as there would be far too many zeros at the end of each number! Instead, astronomers use a measurement called "light years" to measure the distance in space. One light year is equal to the distance that light can travel in one Earth year, which is 6 trillion miles (9.5 trillion km).

Stars are like people – they are born, they live and then they die. But instead of living for 80, 90 or 100 years, as humans do, stars exist for billions of years. The Earth's Sun was born 5 billion years ago, and scientists believe that it is halfway through its life. As it will be another 5 billion years before it dies, no-one living today will see it happen.

Constellations

Astronomers – scientists who study the night sky and everything in it – have created maps of the stars, joining them together in shapes and patterns. These patterns are called "constellations", which comes from a Latin word meaning "set of stars".

Some constellations are enormous and their pattern is easy to spot. Other constellations are very small and made up of faint stars, so they are harder to find.

Once you have learned one or two constellations and know what to look for, they will become familiar and keep you company on clear nights.

Every year, the Earth travels in a big circle around the Sun. This journey is known as an "orbit". As the Earth moves in orbit, the seasons change and new constellations appear. Here are a few to look out for in the night sky:

1. A mighty lion called Leo guards the heavens.

2. Aquila, the beautiful eagle, flies alongside Cygnus, the graceful swan.

3. The magical winged horse Pegasus can be seen in the sky after dark.

4. Orion, the brave hunter with a sword or club, belt and shield, is attacked by the fierce bull Taurus.

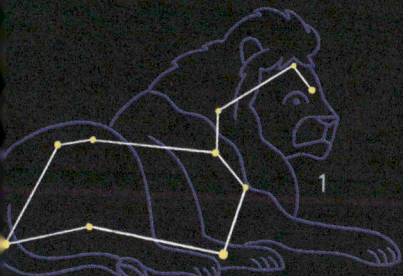

1

2

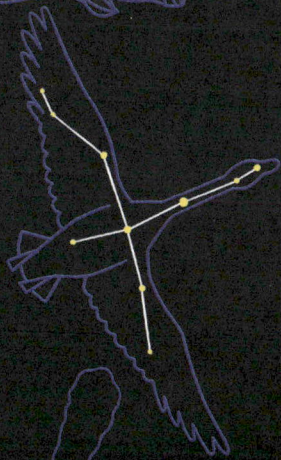

3

4

The Sun

A star lies at the very centre of our solar system – it is what
we call the Sun. Eight planets travel around, or orbit, the Sun.
The Earth might seem huge to the people living on it, but the
Sun is much, much bigger. If it was hollow, the Sun could
hold a million Earths inside it – with plenty of room to spare!

The Sun is vital to all life on Earth, as it provides heat and
light. If the Sun stopped shining, the Earth and everything
on the surface would be plunged into darkness and would
eventually freeze.

Humans should never look directly at the Sun, but scientists
have developed special telescopes to help astronomers study
our closest star. These studies show giant loops of hot gas,
called "prominences", leaping off the Sun's surface. Some of
these loops are so enormous that the Earth could fly through
them, like a ball sailing through a basketball hoop!

Explosions on the Sun's surface blow very hot gas and
energy out into space. These impact the skies on Earth,
causing the night sky in the far north and the far south of the
planet to glow with rippling red-and-green curtains and tall
beams of blue-and-white light. These colourful displays
are known as the "aurora" – in the north they are known
as "aurora borealis" and in the south, "aurora australis".

Neptune

Uranus

Saturn

Jupiter

• Mars

● Earth

● Venus

· Mercury

(Distance not to scale)

WICKLOW COUNTY COUNCIL
LIBRARY SERVICE

Mercury

Mercury is the planet closest to the Sun. It is a relatively small planet, just a little bit bigger than the Earth's Moon. Mercury is covered with thousands of holes, called "craters", which were caused by rocks crashing into its surface long ago.

Mercury orbits the Sun much faster than Earth does. It takes one year, or 365 days, for Earth to travel once round the Sun. Mercury's orbit is only 88 days, so if a human lived on Mercury, they could celebrate their birthday every few months!

Mercury is very close to the Sun, which means that it experiences extreme heat and extreme cold. Its surface temperatures range from as high as 430°C (806°F) to as low as -180°C (-292°F)! This means that Mercury cannot support life. If astronauts were able to land on the planet, they would only see bare rock – no trees, grass or animals.

Even though Mercury can reach blistering temperatures, scientists have discovered ice at the bottom of its deepest craters, where it is hidden from sunlight. This means that water must exist on the planet, even if wildlife does not.

Mercury is so close to the Sun that it is difficult to see from Earth. Humans can only see it occasionally and for a short time, before sunrise or after sunset.

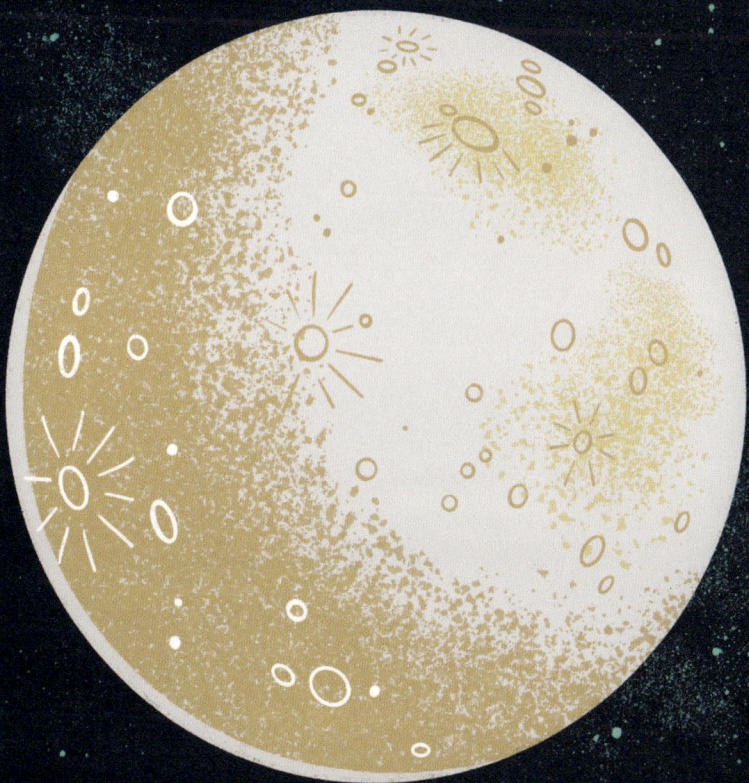

Venus

The second planet from the Sun, Venus, can sometimes be seen from Earth. The best time to look for Venus is before sunrise or after sunset, when the planet appears as a bright, beautiful star. This is why it is sometimes called "the morning star" or "the evening star".

Venus shines so brightly because it is wrapped in thick clouds that reflect sunlight like a mirror. These clouds trap the Sun's heat, creating surface temperatures of over 460°C (860°F). This is so hot that even metals, like lead, would melt instantly if they were to touch the ground.

Venus has been nicknamed "Earth's twin" because the two planets are roughly the same size, but they are very different. On Venus, the air is poisonous, the rain is made of acid and the clouds are thick and heavy. One day, astronauts might be able to float around Venus using specialized airships, but for now only space probes have been able to get close enough to photograph the surface.

If it were possible to visit Venus, the planet would be a gloomy and hazy place. The dense clouds and thick air would make it difficult to see anything, including the Sun. Looking at anything on Venus would be similar to peering through a pair of smeared glasses.

Earth

Earth is the third planet from the Sun and holds a very important position in the solar system. The distance between Earth and its closest star means that the atmosphere on the planet is perfectly balanced and able to support a huge variety of plant and animal life, including humans. If the Earth were any closer to the Sun, its surface temperature would be far too hot for life to exist, and if it were any further away, it would be far too cold.

Life on Earth is also possible because it is the only planet with liquid water on its surface – in fact, water covers 70 per cent of the planet. Ice may have been found on other planets, such as Mercury and Mars, but Earth is the only planet with rivers, lakes and oceans of water. It is also the only planet where water falls from the sky as rain (and the only planet with music, chocolate and Wi-Fi!).

There are other things that make Earth a perfect home. The Moon defends the planet from space rocks, which would cause a huge amount of damage if they were to hit Earth's surface. The Moon is like a giant space goalkeeper! Earth also has a strong magnetic field, which protects us from the harmful radiation of the Sun and deep space. The mixture of different gases in Earth's atmosphere is just right for humans to breathe, too. No other planet that we know of has the same perfect balance.

The Moon

Planets travel around the Sun, but moons orbit planets. The Earth's Moon is a huge ball of rock that travels round the Earth, taking 27 days to complete a single orbit. It is known as Earth's natural satellite and is one quarter of Earth's size.

When looking up at the Moon from Earth, it appears to change shape from night to night. On some nights, it looks like a crescent, and on others it appears as a half or full circle. These different shapes are called "phases", and they are caused by light from the Sun shining on different parts of the Moon as it travels around the Earth.

If you look at the Moon when it is full, you might notice light and dark markings on it. Many people think these markings look like the eyes, nose and mouth of a face, and have come to be called "the man in the moon".

Scientists believe the Moon was created around 4.5 billion years ago when the solar system was still young and a wandering planet smashed into the Earth. The collision threw rocks and dust into space, which became trapped in the Earth's orbit and eventually came together to form the Moon. Other planets have moons as well – Mars has two moons, for example, and Jupiter has more than 70!

1. Full moon
2. Waxing gibbous
3. First quarter
4. Waxing crescent
5. New moon
6. Waning crescent
7. Third quarter
8. Waning gibbous

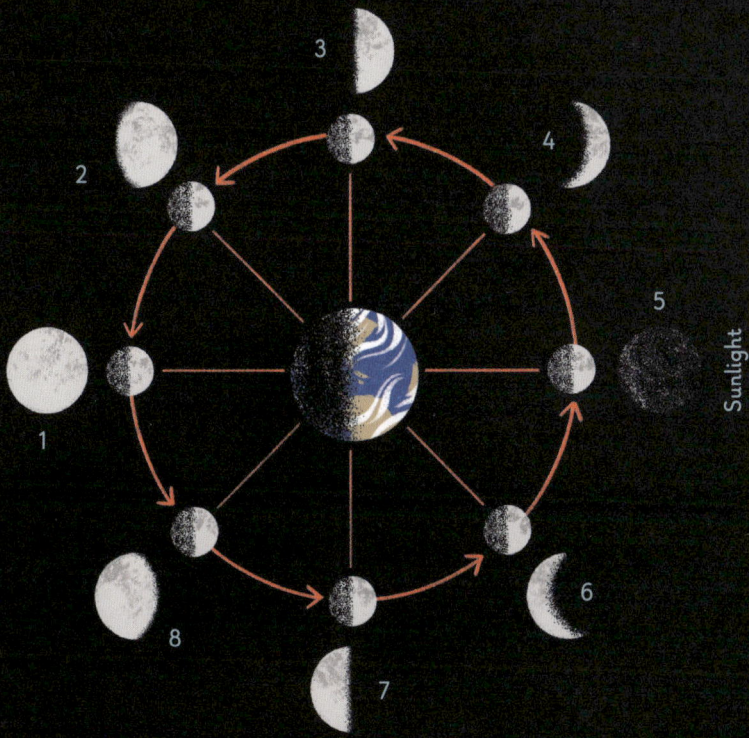

1

2

3

4

5

Sunlight

6

7

8

Mars

Mars is only about half the size of Earth, but it is a little planet with big ideas. It has some of the highest mountains and deepest canyons in the solar system. Olympus Mons, a volcano on Mars, is three times higher than Mount Everest, the highest mountain on Earth. Mars's Mariner Valley is a canyon so long that it would stretch from London to New York, and in some places, it is more than 4.4 miles (7 km) deep!

For centuries, Mars has been nicknamed "the red planet" because it looks, from Earth, like a bright red star in the sky. The vast plains of dust on the planet's surface are the reason behind its famous colour. This dust also turns the sky on Mars a lovely orange-pink colour – similar to some of the sunsets experienced on Earth.

Mars is further away from the Sun than Earth is, which means it is a lot colder. The temperature there can fall below -100°C (-148°F). Although Mars looks like a hot desert planet, it is actually a very cold, dusty world.

Mars is the planet most similar to Earth, which makes it even more fascinating, particularly to astronomers. Although humans are yet to set foot on it, many space probes have photographed Mars from orbit, looking down at its volcanoes, canyons and mountains.

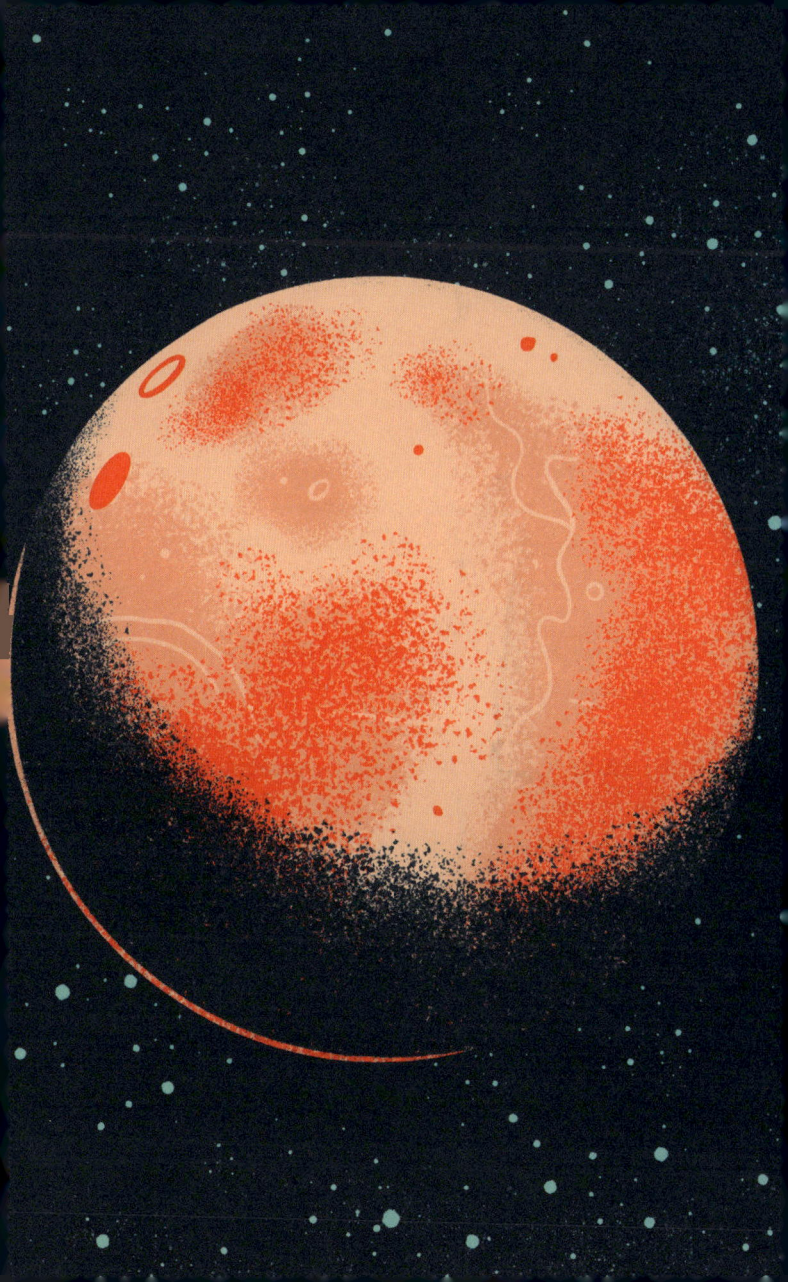

Life on Mars

On 20 July 1976, NASA, the American space programme, successfully landed *Viking 1* on the surface of Mars. Since then, many of these landing probes, known as "rovers", have driven miles across Mars to study the planet and to uncover its secrets.

Rovers have sent thousands of photographs to scientists on Earth. Before their missions ended, the rovers *Spirit* and *Opportunity* crossed deserts, climbed hills and drove into craters. At the time of writing, the current working rover, *Curiosity*, is exploring a crater with a mountain at the centre, which it is due to climb.

Many scientists think that there used to be life on Mars, as studies reveal that it was once a warmer, wetter planet. In the future, rovers will look for fossils in the rocks to discover if this theory is correct. Mars might even be supporting life today, with organisms hiding beneath rocks or deep underground, waiting to be found!

Humans haven't yet invented the rockets and spaceships that astronauts need in order to reach Mars. However, scientists believe that the first explorers to Mars might be walking across the red planet by the year 2040. Perhaps, when you grow up, you will be one of the first humans to fly to Mars in search of life . . .

The asteroid belt

Asteroids are objects made of rock and metal that orbit the Sun like miniature planets. They appear all over the solar system, but a large quantity are found in an area between Mars and Jupiter, known as "the asteroid belt".

Asteroids are all different. Some are many miles wide and others are the size of small boulders. Some asteroids are round and some look more like bowling pins, or two balls that have fused together. Space probes have photographed asteroids, revealing dusty, rock-covered surfaces with features such as craters and hills.

Astronomers think asteroids are pieces of planets that were never formed. Scientists hope to be able to land an astronaut on an asteroid one day – but the astronaut will have to anchor themselves to the surface of the asteroid with strong lines, otherwise they will float off into space!

Sixty-five million years ago, an asteroid smashed into Earth and created an enormous crater off the Yucatán Peninsula in Mexico. The explosion would have filled the sky with dust, blocking out the Sun's light and heat for a long, long time. Many scientists believe that this was the event that killed the dinosaurs. Today, astronomers are always watching for asteroids that might be heading our way, just in case . . .

Jupiter

On clear nights, Jupiter can be seen from Earth, appearing in the sky as a bright yellow-white star. Jupiter is roughly 390 million miles (628 million km) away from Earth, but because it is the largest planet in the whole solar system, we can see it without a telescope. In fact, the only object in the solar system bigger than Jupiter is the Sun.

Jupiter is so huge that it is known as a "gas giant", and the planet could fit roughly 1,300 Earths inside. Unlike the rocky, solid planets closer to the Sun, Jupiter is made of gas. If an astronaut tried to land on Jupiter, they would sink through its clouds until they were squashed into nothing at the planet's solid core.

Jupiter's cloud formations make it a very stormy planet. One particular storm, known as the "Great Red Spot" because of its colour, is twice as wide as Earth itself. It has been blowing for hundreds of years, and the winds on the edge of the storm can reach up to 423 miles per hour (680 km/h) — much stronger than any storm experienced on Earth.

Several space probes have visited Jupiter. Some have raced past without stopping, while others have entered its orbit and studied this vast planet for many years. The American spacecraft *Juno* entered Jupiter's orbit in 2016 to monitor the planet and search for clues about how it was formed.

Jupiter's moons

In many ways, Jupiter is a mini solar system, with 79 known moons circling it like small planets. Jupiter's four largest and most well-known moons are called Io, Europa, Ganymede and Callisto. Galileo Galilei, an Italian astronomer, discovered them in 1610 using one of the first telescopes, so they are known as the "Galilean moons". They can be seen from Earth using binoculars and, together, they look like a chain of tiny, beautiful stars.

Io's yellow-and-red colouring reminds many stargazers of a pizza. It is covered in volcanoes, many of which have been photographed erupting.

Europa has a thick crust of ice, criss-crossed with cracks. There is an ocean of water beneath the crust, where some scientists think forms of alien life might be lurking . . .

Ganymede is a huge ball of dark ice with bright craters. It is the largest moon in the solar system – it's even bigger than the planet Mercury.

Callisto is an icy moon, home to tall, sharp towers of ice, some reaching heights of 100 metres (328 ft).

Saturn

Like Jupiter, Saturn is a gas giant that is mainly made up of the light gases hydrogen and helium. It is so light that if you could find a bathtub big enough, it would float on top of the water, like a huge rubber duck!

As the sixth planet from the Sun, Saturn takes much longer than other planets to complete one orbit. In fact, one full orbit on Saturn lasts 29 Earth years.

Saturn is surrounded by a beautiful system of rings, which look like glowing hoops. Other planets in the solar system have rings, too, but because Saturn's are the biggest and best, it is nicknamed "the ringed planet".

When viewed through a telescope, Saturn's rings look solid, but they are actually made from millions of floating rock particles, pieces of dust and chunks of ice. Space probes have visited Saturn and found that the large hoops are made up of thousands of individual rings.

For a long time, it was thought that Saturn's rings were formed billions of years ago, when one or more moons were destroyed in Saturn's orbit, and the remaining pieces of moon came together to form the rings. However, recent scientific evidence suggests that the rings may not be as old as scientists first thought. So the mystery continues . . .

Uranus

Uranus is the Sun's closest ice giant – a planet made up of ice and gas instead of rock and metal. The combination of methane and other gases in its clouds has turned the planet a mysterious blue-green colour. Uranus can appear as a tiny green star in the night sky. It is very faint, and most people need binoculars or a telescope to see it.

Uranus is an exceptionally cold planet because it is so far away from the Sun. As it sits within the outer solar system, light from the Sun takes 2 hours and 40 minutes to reach Uranus, and the temperature in the icy clouds can fall to lower than -200°C (-328°F).

Unlike all the other planets, which spin upright round the Sun like spinning tops, Uranus rolls around the Sun on its side like a barrel. Astronomers think another celestial body slammed into Uranus and knocked it over a long time ago, causing it to spin sideways!

Only one spacecraft has ever visited Uranus. In 1986, NASA's *Voyager 2* flew past Uranus and took photographs of its light and dark clouds. *Voyager 2* also photographed tall cliffs and strange v-shaped markings on the surface of Miranda, one of Uranus's 27 moons. Astronomers think these markings might have been caused by a meteorite smashing into Miranda long ago.

Neptune

Neptune is also an ice giant in the outer region of the solar system. It is the last known planet of the solar system and sits almost 3.1 billion miles (5 billion km) from the Sun. Neptune can only be seen from Earth through a telescope and takes 165 Earth years to complete one orbit – in 2011, Neptune completed its first full orbit since discovery in 1846!

The planet does not have a solid surface, although it is thought to have a rocky core at the centre. Most of Neptune's surface is made up of "icy", fluid materials – including water, methane and ammonia.

Telescopes and space probes have photographed Neptune's violent storms. The planet hosts winds that rage at over 1,500 miles per hour (2,400 km/h) – the fastest in the whole solar system. These storms are caused by heat swells from beneath Neptune's clouds.

Like Uranus, Neptune has a small family of icy moons – fourteen have been discovered so far. Triton, Neptune's largest moon, has geysers on its pink, icy surface, which spray jets of dark, dusty material high into the sky.

Neptune has a system of dark, narrow rings, but they are difficult to see from Earth. Only one space probe, *Voyager 2*, has seen them up close.

Pluto and the dwarf planets

When Pluto was first discovered in 1930, scientists decided that it was a planet. But in 2006, modern astronomers disagreed with this. They argued that the existence of other large celestial objects near Pluto meant that the planet did not have a big enough presence within its orbit. As a result, Pluto was declared to be a dwarf planet instead.

When the space probe *New Horizons* flew past Pluto in 2015, it took photographs that amazed astronomers back on Earth. Scientists had thought Pluto to be a boring planet, but the photos showed towering mountains, deep craters, winding canyons and a huge centre of pink-white ice.

Pluto's moon, Charon, is particularly characterful. Many areas on its surface have been named after characters and places from science fiction. If you were to visit, you could meet Dorothy from *The Wizard of Oz*, Darth Vader and Captain Kirk before exploring Mordor (from *The Lord of the Rings*) and Gallifrey, the home of Doctor Who!

Other dwarf planets have been found even further away from the Sun than Pluto, such as Makemake and Eris. Makemake is estimated to be only 900 miles (1,450 km) wide and takes over 300 years to orbit the Sun. Eris is larger, and it is 68 times further from the Sun than Earth is. That's so far away that a year on Eris lasts 557 Earth years!

Comets

As well as eight major planets, hundreds of moons and millions of asteroids, the solar system contains thousands of comets. These dark, icy objects orbit the Sun like huge icebergs in space. Comets have existed since the birth of the solar system. By studying them, scientists can learn a lot about how planets were formed and how the solar system has changed over time.

Even through powerful telescopes, comets look like tiny fuzzy stars. But as they pass the Sun, they warm up, releasing gas and dust into space. Some comets grow long, beautiful tails and can be seen in the night sky, appearing as starlike objects with glowing tails stretching behind them.

Space probes have studied several comets up close and, in 2014, the small probe *Philae* even landed on one. From this, scientists learned that comets have cliffs, craters, landslides and boulders on their dusty surfaces.

The most famous comet is Halley's Comet. It orbits the Sun once every 76 years. Chinese astronomers recorded the first known sighting of Halley's Comet in 239 BCE, but it was the English astronomer Edmond Halley who first noticed and understood the comet's orbit around the Sun. His discovery was then recognized in the naming of the newly discovered comet.

The Milky Way and beyond

The solar system is enormous, but it is only a tiny part of the wider universe. The Sun is just one star in a giant spiral of thousands of millions of stars in a galaxy called "the Milky Way". Its name came from the ancient Greeks and Romans, who decided that it looked like spilled milk in the sky.

Our galaxy whirls around like a Catherine wheel, but it is so enormous that a single rotation takes around 250 million years. We are able to see the Milky Way from Earth. It looks like a band of misty smoke to the naked eye, but when viewed through binoculars or a telescope, you can see that it is made up of millions of faint, faraway stars.

Astronomers have found planets orbiting more than 4,000 other stars in the Milky Way, so it is certain that our solar system isn't the only one in existence. There may be billions of solar systems like this one in outer space.

The Milky Way isn't the only galaxy, either. For every star in our galaxy, there is another galaxy out in space with billions of stars of its own, probably with their own planets and solar systems, too. Is there life out there? Well, scientists aren't sure. But if there isn't, it would be a huge waste of space, wouldn't it?

A Ladybird Book

collectable books for curious kids

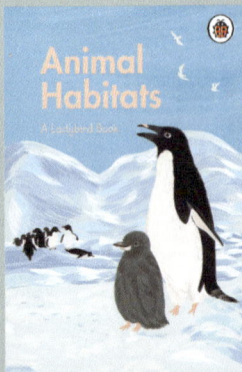

Animal Habitats

9780241416860

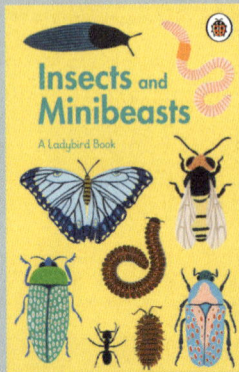

Insects and Minibeasts

9780241417034

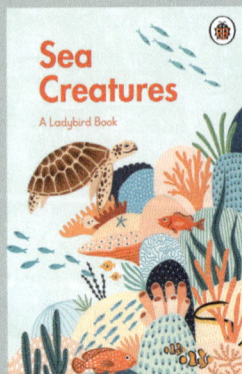

Sea Creatures

9780241417072

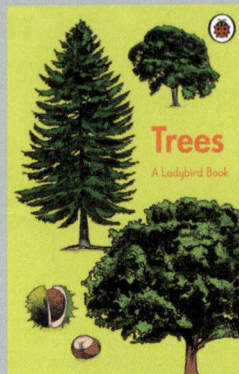

Trees

9780241417218

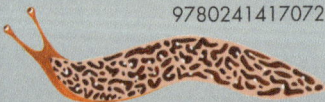

SERIES 208

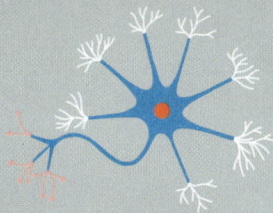

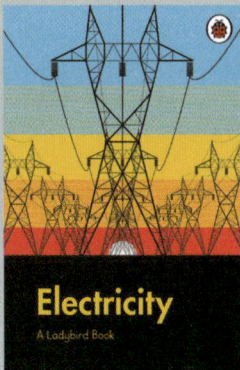

Electricity

9780241416945

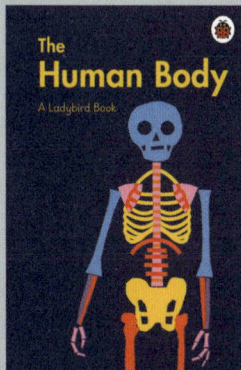

The Human Body

9780241416983

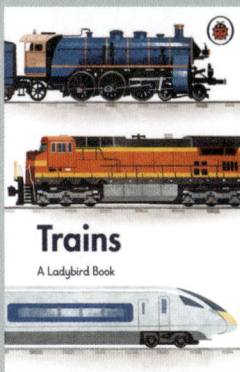

Trains

9780241417171

Weather

9780241417362

SÉRIES 218